W9-DFM-205

animals**animals**

Vultures

by **Renee C. Rebman**

Marshall Cavendish
Benchmark

New York

Special thanks to Donald E. Moore III, associate director of animal care at the Smithsonian Institution's National Zoo, for his expert reading of this manuscript.

Published by Marshall Cavendish Benchmark
An imprint of Marshall Cavendish Corporation

Other Marshall Cavendish Offices:
Marshall Cavendish International (Asia) Private Limited, 1 New Industrial Road, Singapore 536196
• Marshall Cavendish International (Thailand) Co Ltd. 253 Asoke, 12th Flr, Sukhumvit 21 Road, Klongtoey Nua, Wattana, Bangkok 10110, Thailand • Marshall Cavendish (Malaysia) Sdn Bhd, Times Subang, Lot 46, Subang Hi-Tech Industrial Park, Batu Tiga, 40000 Shah Alam, Selangor Darul Ehsan, Malaysia

Marshall Cavendish is a trademark of Times Publishing Limited

All websites were available and accurate when this book was sent to press.

Rebman, Renee C., 1961-
Vultures / by Renee C. Rebman.
p. cm.
Summary: "Provides comprehensive information on the anatomy, special skills, habitats, and diet of vultures"—Provided by publisher.
Includes index.
ISBN 978-0-7614-4880-8 (print)
ISBN 978-1-60870-621-1 (ebook)
1. Vultures—Juvenile literature. I. Title.
QL696.F32R43 2012
598.9'2—dc22
2010016037

Photo research by Joan Meisel

Cover photo: Top-Picks TBK/Alamy

The photographs in this book are used by permission and through the courtesy of:
Alamy: Krys Bailey, 1; David Tipling, 4; blickwinkel, 12; Wayne Lynch, 15; B.A.E. Inc.,18; Juanvi Carrasco, 21; All Canada Photos, 25; Maximilian Weinzierl, 29; Nick Hanna, 37; Peter Arnold, Inc., 41. *Corbis*: O. Alamany & E. Vicens, 26. *Getty Images*: 18th Dynasty Egyptian, 7; Wener Bollmann, 11(r); Theo Allofs, 11(l); Frank Lukasseck, 22; Tom Ulrich, 30; AFP, 39. *Minden Pictures*: Neil Bowman, 34. *Photolibrary*: Bios/Peter Arnold, Inc., 33. *Stockphoto Pro*: Krys Bailey/Marmotta Photo Art. 17.

Editor: Joy Bean
Publisher: Michelle Bisson
Art Director: Anahid Hamparian
Series Designer: Adam Mietlowski

Printed in Malaysia (T)
1 3 5 6 4 2

Contents

Scavengers of the Earth

A vulture glides gracefully through the sky, circling on strong currents of wind. Its sharp eyes search the ground below for its next meal. The scent of rotting meat is detected by the vulture's highly developed sense of smell. A large groundhog lies motionless beside a nearby ditch.

The vulture descends and lands within a few feet of the groundhog. Walking around the animal several times, the vulture makes certain it is dead before hopping on top and digging into the tasty flesh. Very soon, other vultures will surely detect the feast and join in to claim their portion. When the vultures are done eating their meal, nothing will be left of the groundhog but bits of bone.

Vultures glide on the wind as they look for food from the air.

Vultures are *scavengers,* which means they do not hunt and kill their food. They survive by eating *carrion*—the flesh of dead animals. Because of this, vultures are associated with death and disease. Many people find them unclean, and even unlucky. Some people feel that a nearby vulture is a bad omen. But history shows this was not always the case.

Many ancient cultures have considered vultures to be an important part of their folklore and beliefs. Their images appear in art and sculptures. The Egyptians felt the birds were so important that two of their goddesses, Mut and Nekhbet, were depicted as having vulture heads. Nekhbet was considered the guardian of mothers and children. The image of Nekhbet was featured in a large gold necklace found on the mummy of the famous boy pharaoh Tutankhamen (also known as King Tut). The solid gold mask that covered the pharaoh's face also had the head of a vulture depicted next to that of a cobra. Images of the vulture goddesses have been found on many Egyptian coffins and in the artwork on the walls of the tombs. These findings show how important the vulture goddesses were to their culture.

A vulture head can be see on this mask of King Tut.

Native Americans of the western coast of the United States used vulture feathers during many of their important ceremonies. They believed thunder came from the powerful flapping of the wings of the California condor, one of the world's largest vultures. People of the Chumash tribe feel they are so closely linked to the condor that if the bird ever becomes extinct, their tribe will die out as well.

Other cultures also held strong beliefs about vultures. Ancient Incas believed they were messengers of the gods. In India it was believed vultures guarded the gates to the underworld. Vultures throughout the ages have been associated with magical powers, perhaps because of their natural behavior of dealing with death on a daily basis without coming to harm.

Fossils indicate that prehistoric vultures first appeared on Earth 40 to 50 million years ago. This means that ancient vultures fed off of the great prehistoric mammals that existed, such as the mastodon and woolly mammoth. Vulture survival depended on following the prehistoric grazing animals, such as wild cattle, deer, and antelope. As these species grew and flourished, so did vultures.

Vultures belong to the group of birds called Falconiformes. There are twenty-two species of vultures in the world. They are split into two groups: the Old World and the New World vultures. Scientists believe that Old and New World vultures developed separately from different ancestors. This is known as *convergent* evolution.

There are seven New World vultures, which include two types of condors, the California and the Andean. These vultures are all related to storks. They live in the western *hemisphere* of the world from southern Canada down to the tip of South America.

Old World vultures live in Africa, Europe, and Asia. There are fourteen species that are descended from birds of prey such as eagles and buzzards. Over many thousands of years, vultures have lost the ability to hunt and kill.

Today, vultures make their home on every continent except Antarctica. Although they live in different parts of the world, Old World and New World vultures share many similar behaviors and distinct looks that set them apart from all other birds.

Species Chart

◆ There are seven species of New World vultures, including turkey vultures, Andean condors, black vultures, and California condors. The Andean condor is the largest of the New World vultures and has the largest wingspan of any living bird (9 feet or 3 m). It is also the heaviest flying bird in the world. This vulture can grow to be 4 feet (1.2 m) tall and weigh up to 33 pounds (15 kilograms).

◆ There are fourteen species of Old World vultures, including monk vultures, bearded vultures, hooded vultures, and white-headed vultures. The hooded vulture is the smallest of the Old World vultures. It grows to be just 2.5 feet (76 centimeters) tall and weighs up to 4.5 pounds (2 kg). Its wingspan is 5 feet (1.5 m).

This black vulture is a member of a New World species.

The hooded vulture, such as this one, is an Old World species.

2 Anatomy of a Vulture

To most people's eyes, vultures are odd-looking birds. Their beady eyes, bald head, and hooked beaks make a bad first impression to most people. Their entire body is built for survival. This design has certainly worked, considering how long vultures have roamed the earth.

One of vultures' most recognizable features is their distinctive bald heads. Their bare heads are very convenient for them. While feeding, vultures plunge their heads deep into the carrion. Their head and long neck become covered in blood and bits of flesh. If their heads had feathers, they could not keep them clean. Their bald heads also reduce the risk of picking up *parasites*, which could make the animal sick.

Vultures are recognizable because of their bald heads and beady eyes.

Many vultures have bumpy flesh-colored skulls, but some vultures' heads are brightly colored in red, orange, or yellow. Sometimes they are several colors. In contrast, their bodies are more neutral in color, with feathers of white, brown, or black.

Both male and female vultures are similar in weight and size. All vultures, no matter what their size, have a wide wingspan. The Egyptian vulture weighs less than 5 pounds (2.2 kg) and is only 24 inches (61 cm) long, yet it has a wingspan of 5.7 feet (1.7 m). The largest vulture, the Andean condor, weighs 33 pounds (15 kilograms) and is 4 feet (1.2 m) long. Its wingspan is an amazing 10.5 feet (3.2 m). It is one of the largest birds on Earth that is capable of flying.

Vultures have sharp-edged hooked beaks that are designed to easily tear at the flesh they eat. Their beaks are made of material similar to human fingernails, only much thicker and stronger. The Egyptian vulture has a thin, narrow beak that enables it to extract the marrow from bones.

Vultures have short legs and *talons* that help them grasp their food while they tear at the flesh. New

The talons on a vulture are not very strong.

World vultures, which are not descended from birds of prey, have weaker talons and beaks than Old World vultures.

All vultures have excellent eyesight. They can spot carrion from high in the sky. New World vultures also have a highly developed sense of smell. These vultures live in areas covered with trees. It is not possible for them to see some carrion through the thick foliage. As carrion begins to rot, New World vultures pick up the scent, which guides them to their dinner.

Another interesting fact about vultures is that they cannot sing like other birds. They have no *syrinx* (voice box). Vultures hiss, wheeze, or cackle to communicate. They make these noises by blowing air through their noses. A group of vultures feasting on carrion can make quite a bit of noise.

Vultures, like most birds, have no bladder. They do not store their waste. They get rid of it by excreting frequently throughout the day. The white sticky excrement is called guano. Vultures also have no sweat glands. They will urinate on their own legs to cool off. This action also kills any germs they may have picked up while walking through carrion.

When a vulture feels threatened by another bird or animal, the vulture will stomp its feet to send the message to stay away. If it still feels threatened, it will project vomit at the enemy. A vulture can expel vomit a distance of 6 feet (1.8 m). The vomit has a high acid content and is extremely smelly. Most animals soon learn it is best just to leave a vulture alone.

Despite these distasteful habits, vultures are clean birds. They often bathe in rivers

Did You Know . . .
The lammergeyer vulture has a special trick for getting to the insides of the bones they want to eat. They wait until other vultures have picked a *carcass* clean, then they grab a bone, fly high in the air, and drop it to break it open. They then pick the marrow from inside the bone.

and lakes. To dry off, they stand in the sunshine with their wings stretched out.

From the tip of their curved beaks to the end of their short tails, vultures have many unique features. They may not be very popular, but they are among the most interesting birds on Earth.

This Egyptian vulture has a large hook on the end of its beak that helps it tear at its food.

3 Flight and Feeding

Soaring through the sky, vultures are quite majestic. Their bodies are objects of grace and examples of efficiency. Vultures have mastered the art of flying using the least amount of effort.

Their wings are broad and large in comparison to their body size. This enables the vulture to use the wind to its advantage and allows it to glide for long distances. Because most vultures are big birds, they need help to get into the sky. Some vultures living among high hills jump off them to catch the wind underneath their wings. Others depend on *thermal upcurrents* to become airborne.

Thermal upcurrents occur when the sun heats the ground and a patch of warm air develops. This warm

Vultures will circle around an area together searching for food.

air is thicker than the surrounding cooler air, so the warmer air begins to rise. The air inside the thermal current spins as it lifts, while the air outside the thermal current sinks downward.

Vultures position themselves inside the rising air and circle inside it as the warm air climbs higher and higher. In Africa, strong thermal currents can lift a vulture to 15,000 feet (4,572 m) or more. Once the vulture reaches a high altitude, it flies out of the thermal and begins to glide.

As the bird glides, it naturally loses altitude, but vultures can remain in the air without flapping their wings for amazing distances. Vultures sometimes need to glide for miles before finding food. It is not uncommon for a vulture to travel 200 miles (321.8 km) per day. Some vultures can glide for up to six hours without flapping their wings. Gliding requires very little effort. This preserves their energy.

Vultures must also preserve heat. The air at higher altitudes is cooler. To help keep warm, many vultures, such as the turkey vulture, keep their heads tucked in toward their feathered collars. They fly holding

Did You Know . . .
Turkey vultures are easy to spot as they glide through the sky. They rock from side to side as they fly and hold their wings in a shallow V shape. When perched, these birds often sit with their wings partly open, giving them a distinct appearance. They *roost* together in large groups.

This bearded vulture glides through the sky. It does not have to flap its wings too often, which saves energy.

When vultures are about to land, they will hold out their legs to touch down on the ground.

their wings in a slight V formation instead of straight out to the sides. The bird rides gently on the air currents using the feathers at the tips of its wings for control.

Some vultures fly and hunt for food in small groups, but others hunt alone. Once a vulture spots something promising to eat, it glides to the ground, sticking out its short legs like landing gear just before touchdown. If another vulture spots this action, it will

22

be sure to follow. No vulture ever gets to dine alone. Before long it will be joined by other vultures trying to claim their own portion of the meal.

Vultures do not just dive into their dinner. They usually walk around the carcass a few times to make certain it is dead. The animal may have died from old age, disease, or accident. A carcass that had been dead for too long will be left alone. Vultures enjoy fresh meat.

Once a vulture decides to eat, it will hop right on top of the carcass and begin to dig in. It braces its feet against the carcass and uses its beak to tear flesh. It usually begins at a soft spot such as the eyes, or if it can rip open the flesh, it eats the internal organs. If the flesh is tough, it is common for two or more vultures to grab on to the meat with their talons. They then flap their wings, propelling themselves backward to pull it apart.

There is a feeding order among vultures. The large vultures eat first. Once they have gorged themselves on the innards, the smaller vultures move in to eat the remaining meat scraps off the bone. Carrion can attract many vultures. A dead antelope can feed more than twenty vultures, while a dead elephant can feed more than one hundred.

Most animals cannot eat the rotting flesh of dead animals because viruses or bacteria in the carrion could make them sick. Vultures, however, are able to eat rotting flesh because they have strong digestive juices that make the rotten flesh harmless to their digestive systems. Their stomach acids are so strong few viruses or bacteria survive. If vultures are hungry and no meat is available, they will also eat eggs or rotting vegetables.

Like most birds, vultures have a *crop* (food pouch) that stores excess food. Depending upon the size of the vulture, a little more than 3 pounds (1.3 kg) of food can be stored. In just ten minutes, a vulture can fill its crop so full it bulges.

Vultures have a low *metabolism*. This means their bodies are so efficient they burn little energy. This helps the bird survive even if little food is available. Vultures can go for a week between meals.

Vultures spend their days flying and feeding. They do both in amazing and efficient ways.

*This vulture's crop is
full from a big meal.*

The Life Cycle of a Vulture

Mating seasons for vultures vary depending on how warm the *climate* is where they live. Generally, the mating season begins in March. When male vultures look for a mate, they show off their flying skills by circling close to the female. They hiss and wheeze to try and get her attention. If the female is interested, she will fly off with a male. In the air they will chase each other and circle around and around. Some species pair up and mate for life. Others stay together just long enough to raise their chick. After mating they look for a suitable place to nest.

New World vultures do not build nests. They pick a suitable spot to lay their eggs, such as a cave or hollowed-out tree. Sometimes they take over an old,

This New World vulture has chosen a spot in a cliffside to care for her young.

27

abandoned nesting place. Some species, such as the black vulture, simply lay their eggs on the ground. Turkey vultures are a little more social than most vultures. They choose nesting sites near a community roost, or gathering place, of other turkey vultures. Their individual nesting places are usually scratched out of the ground.

Old World vultures build nests out of branches. Choosing a place to nest is left up to the female. Vultures like to nest close to other vultures but not too close. If another vulture ventures too near, it will be chased away. Once a place is chosen, the male brings material to the site, and the female does most of the work of building the nest. The lappet-faced vultures build very large nests up to 9 feet (2.7 m) across.

A female vulture will sometimes lay two eggs per *clutch*, but many species only lay one egg. This egg must be kept warm for the chick to develop. Both the female and male vulture take turns sitting on the egg. One will watch over the egg while the other hunts for food. If they are bothered by a *predator* while watching the nest, they will hiss and charge at the intruder to try and frighten it away. If that does not work, they will project their vomit or excrete waste to try and get

This Old World vulture has created a nest on the top of a tree in Africa.

rid of the intruder, but they will not abandon the nest.

In warmer climates the egg will hatch after twenty-eight days. In colder climates it may take up to fifty-six days for the egg to hatch. A newborn chick weighs about 2 ounces (56.7 grams). It is born with soft downy feathers, and its eyes are open. Once out of its shell, the tiny chick is completely dependent on its parents.

Two black vulture chicks rest together in their nest.

Vulture chicks are very vulnerable to predators such as skunks, foxes, and raccoons. Chicks cannot protect themselves and are in great danger if left alone. They also cannot regulate their own body temperature. They depend on their parents to keep them warm. They need constant care for the first five days of life.

Vulture parents feed their chick with *regurgitated* food brought up from their crops. The chick will push its head into the parent's throat to feed. Chicks from larger vulture species need up to 28 ounces (0.8 kg) of food per day. Adults can get by with 15 ounces (0.4 kg) per day. They usually have plenty of stored food left over for the chick. When the chick gets a few weeks older, the parents will bring it small pieces of meat to eat. If food is scarce and there are two chicks in a nest, the stronger chick may kill its weaker sibling in order to survive.

After about two weeks, the parents will leave the nest for short periods of time. When a parent returns to the nest, it lands

Did You Know . . .
If the eggs are stolen from a black vulture's nest, the female will lay a second pair of eggs (known as a clutch) within three weeks in a different nest. This behavior is known as double clutching. Other species of vultures also double clutch.

nearby but does not approach it immediately. It will walk around for about fifteen minutes to see if any predator is watching before it joins the chick.

Chicks do not learn to fly until they are at least ten weeks old. Andean condors do not fly until they are six months old. By five to six months of age vultures begin going with their parents to hunt for food. They are soon self-sufficient and ready to live on their own. Condors generally stay with their parents the longest, until they are two years of age.

Vultures in the wild live to be about thirty-eight years old. In captivity they live slightly longer, to about forty-two years of age. The California condor can live longer, up to sixty years of age in the wild.

Mother vultures feed their young by putting food in their mouths.

An Uncertain Future

Vultures play an important role in the cycle of life. They are the natural garbage removal experts of the earth. Dead animals attract disease-carrying insects. If the vultures did not eat this carrion, disease would spread. The land and water supply would become polluted with bodies. This would eventually make farming land unusable and living space uninhabitable.

In some areas of India and Africa, vultures are welcomed and live right in the center of the cities. They scavenge at the town dumping sites and devour the waste at the harbors left from the fishing boats. These city-dwelling vultures have become dependent

Vultures can help a crowded area stay clean by eating garbage that would normally sit and rot.

on humans for their food, and the humans depend on the vultures to take care of their waste. The system is beneficial to both.

However, vultures have also faced many problems caused by humans. In the 1940s the popular poison *DDT* was widely used to kill insects that threatened crops. When vultures ate carcasses of animals that had consumed the poisoned insects, the poison got into the vultures' bodies. Poisoned vultures produced eggs with very thin shells. The eggs often broke before they hatched. Many vultures also died from the poison in their bodies. This means the vulture population was drastically reduced. DDT was banned in the United States in 1972, and the vulture population began to increase.

But in other areas of the world, vultures faced even more dangers from humans. The cape vultures of South Africa depended on the carcasses from large ranches for food. Some ranchers did not want the birds around their livestock, fearing they would spread disease. They shot the birds and began removing dead carcasses off their ranches before the vultures could eat them. This robbed the vultures of their food supply. Cape vultures also extracted calcium

A large number of vultures have died over the years by eating food poisoned
by pesticides. Some pesticides are distributed by airplane. This allows a
large area to be covered with pesticides in a short period of time.

from the bones of dead animals. With a poor food supply, unhealthy chicks were born with deformed legs and wings due to calcium deficiency.

In the United States, land development destroyed nesting sites and hunting grounds of the California condor. The condors were forced to live in a small area of the San Joaquin valley.

This type of condor lays only a single egg every two years, so it reproduces at a very slow rate. If it is disturbed or frightened, it will abandon the nest for hours, leaving the egg or newly hatched chick in danger. The number of California condors rapidly declined.

By 1981 only nineteen condors were left in the wild. Conservationists began trying to save the condor, and the California Condor Recovery Team was formed in 1982. The team would take eggs from wild nests, thus forcing the condor to double clutch. This method was ultimately successful, forcing some pairs to produce up to three eggs in one season.

The team also used *captive breeding*. They captured vultures to use specifically

As part of a captive breeding program, a chick is fed by a hand puppet (on right) that is made to look like an adult vulture.

for breeding and brought them to the Los Angeles Zoo and San Diego's Wild Animal Park. The plan was to raise the chicks and eventually release them back into the wild. Raising the chicks proved to be a little tricky.

The eggs were placed in incubators and carefully monitored. Once the chicks hatched, they had to be fed. Team members fed them by using hand puppets. These puppets were made to look like condors. This method was used to stop the chicks from imprinting on humans. Condors can develop an attraction to humans. This behavior can be detrimental once they are returned to the wild because they will depend on humans for food and shelter. The team knew the chicks had to learn to interact with other vultures.

In 1992, the team decided it was time to release two vultures raised in the program into the wild. They were released in Ventura County, California. Eventually the California Condor Recovery Team released condors in other areas of California, Arizona, and Mexico. It is estimated that there are now more than 140 California condors living in the wild. Even though the program has proved successful, the condors still must try to survive while their *habitat* is being developed and taken over.

All types of vultures still face an uncertain future. Destruction of their natural habitat is the worst problem. Some vultures are killed by pollution after

A California condor is released into the wild after being raised in a captive breeding program.

accidentally ingesting trash and poisons such as antifreeze. Spills of crude oil and other toxins have also entered their food supply.

Vultures are protected by the Migratory Bird Treaty, and it is illegal to kill them in North America. However, they are still being hunted and killed to a small degree all over the world. A large majority of species of vultures are considered to be *endangered*. Like most endangered species, their greatest enemies are humans.

Glossary

abandon—To desert or leave.

captive breeding—The process of breeding animals in human controlled environments, such as zoos and wildlife preserves.

carcass—The body of a dead animal.

carrion—Dead animals that scavengers eat.

climate—Weather conditions in a certain place.

clutch—The set of eggs laid at one time.

convergent—Moving toward the same point in development.

crop—The sacklike part of a bird's digestive track where food is stored.

DDT—A poison used to kill pests that is harmful to animals and is now illegal in the United States.

endangered—Something that is threatened with extinction.

habitat—The place where an animal or

plant naturally exists.

hemisphere—One half of the earth, either northern or southern part.

metabolism—The process by which food is handled in the body.

parasite—An animal that lives on another animal, usually causing it harm.

predator—An animal that hunts and kills other animals for food.

regurgitate—To cough up undigested food to feed young.

roost—A specific place, such as a tree, where birds rest.

scavengers—An animal or other organism that feeds on dead organic matter.

syrinx—The voice box of a bird.

talon—The claw on the toes of a bird.

thermal upcurrent—A rising column of warm air.

Find Out More

Books

Lundgren, Julie K. *Vultures*. Vero Beach, Florida: Rourke Publishing, 2009.

Macken, JoAnn Early. *Vultures*. New York: Gareth Stevens, 2009.

Magellan, Marta. *Those Voracious Vultures*. Sarasota, Florida: Pineapple Publishing, 2008.

Markle, Sandra. *Vultures*. New York: Lerner, 2006.

Websites

The Peregrine Fund
www.peregrinefund.org/explore_raptors/
vultures/vultmain.html

Science Encyclopedia—Vultures
http://science.jrank.org/pages/7270/Vultures.
html

The Turkey Vulture Society
http://vulturesociety.homestead.com

Index

Page numbers for illustrations are in **boldface**.

About the Author

Renee C. Rebman has published more than a dozen nonfiction books for young readers. Her Marshall Cavendish titles include *Anteaters, Turtles and Tortoises, Cows, Cats, Walruses, Rats,* and *How Do Tornadoes Form?* She is also a published playwright. Her plays have been produced in schools and community theaters across the country.